Shield
of Faith

Shield of Faith

by Roy Z. Kemp

Designed by Gordon G. Brown

Published by The C. R. Gibson Company

Dedication

To The Cartledge Families
Hammond, Mildred, Linda,
Ricky, Becky, Angelia
With Love and Affection

Contents

The Shield of Faith

*"Above all, taking the shield of faith,
wherewith ye shall be able to quench
all the fiery darts of the wicked."*

Ephesians 6:16

Faith is a simple word, yet it is frequently misused and misunderstood. True faith is faith in God the Father, the Son and the Holy Spirit. It is a gift of God. And He who gave it will also sustain it. It is faith in Christ's redeeming work. Word and sacrament are the means of grace; they are the channels by which God the Holy Spirit strengthens and builds up a living faith which is active in good works.

"You must have faith" and "You must believe" are phrases we often hear, but to many they have lost their true meaning. Faith is simply believing and trusting in God's love and promises. Faith is knowing Jesus and accepting Him as our Lord and Saviour.

Faith without Christ is nothing. Faith in Christ is everything.

Faith is the link which holds us close to God and through which we receive His love and peace. All of God's loving power becomes ours through a simple trust in Him. In Romans 1:17 we are told: "The just shall live by faith." Because God is faithful to us, we too should be faithful and loyal to him.

Jesus Christ is the Good News of our salvation. Through His innocent suffering, His death on the cross and His resurrection from the grave, He has redeemed us and all lost and condemned mankind from sin, death and the power of the evil one. If we believe and place our trust in His atoning work, we have the assurance of the forgiveness of our sins and of life everlasting.

"God, give me the courage to speak what I truly believe," is a short personal prayer which each and everyone of us might take to heart and express often. "We know that all things work together for good to them that love God, to them who are the called according to His purpose." Romans 8:28.

By placing our faith and trust in Jesus Christ as our Saviour, God's Holy Spirit will provide a shield of faith. Thus we will become His instruments in guiding the weak and leading others to faith.

The blessings of God pour in on us every day. The mercies of God are new every morning. "The Lord is gracious, and full of compassion; slow to anger, and of great mercy. The Lord is good to all: and his tender mercies are over all his works." Psalm 145: 8-9.

The Lord is good to us, and our hearts tell us that we do not deserve the benefits and His blessings. We are unworthy of them. But God loved us so much that He gave His only Son into death that we might live. "What shall I render unto the Lord for all his benefits toward me?" the Psalmist asks in Psalm 116:12.

If we serve God with our whole hearts, we will be fitting temples of the Holy Spirit. God will not ask more from us. Our hearts—our lives—these we are to render to Him for all His benefits to us.

As Christians, we are on the witness stand every minute of every day. We must know the truth and bear witness to it. May we so love the Lord that we will willingly dedicate our lives to witnessing for Him. Acts 1:8 tell us; "Ye shall be witnesses unto me ... unto the uttermost part of the earth."

Each bearer of the shield of faith, doing the Lord's work, must remember that there is no limit to the potential of a man when he moves forward with Jesus Christ as his leader. One in whom the Spirit of Christ dwells is always ready to perform even the lowly task, and has the faith to walk humbly and openly in duty's way.

Jesus is our pattern. Jesus is our ideal and guide. We each should know that to invite and encourage the growth of His Spirit within us is to enhance the richness and the beauty of our lives.

May each of us go forward with faith!

The Shield of Faith

Who bears within his hand the shield of faith,
Who wears God's helmet, bears His fiery spear,
May go a conqueror through any land,
On any day, from year to passing year.

Though dark, tumultuous wars may strongly wage
Against the fighters of our God and Lord,
The shield of faith will be victorious,
For none can slay the brightness of God's Word.

Faith's Dimensions

Faith should be unfailing.
Overcoming every wrong,
Faith has length and breadth and height,
Is steady and is strong.

The length of faith encircles
The future and the past
And links them with the present.
Such faith will last and last.

The breadth of faith is measured
By loving care for others,
Those near at hand, those far away;
All men must be as brothers.

The height of faith goes upward;
Faith spirals from below
And climbs its way to Heaven
From where all mercies flow.

What Faith Is

Faith is a pure white flame
That burns incessantly,
Destroying doubts and fears
And growing constantly.

Faith is my guiding staff.
It helps to make me strong.
I lean on it and rest
When ways are hard and long.

Faith will provide my needs.
Faith will help me attain
All of my aims and dreams.
Faith is my heart's refrain.

Faith will restore my soul.
Faith is my helpful rod.
Faith is my strength and shield.
Faith is belief in God.

Faith in Tomorrow

We know not what the future holds
None can know what comes tomorrow;
It may bring peace and love and joy,
Or it may bring pain and sorrow.

We each must live with faith and hope
And with a heart that understands
That God will furnish every need.
He holds our future in His hands.

Faith

Faith
is that quality within
that enables us
to reach out and grasp
the unseen hand of God.

Faith
is the link
by which the Christian
holds on to the hand
of God and receives
His love and peace.

Faith
is a gift of God.
He who gives it
will preserve it.

Faith
is the root of all blessings.
No miracle will ever come
to a man who does not believe
in miracles.

Faith
permits a person
to go farther than he can see.
Faith will brighten
the darkest way.

A living faith
is active in good works.
A faith is never so beautiful
as when it is wearing
its working clothes.

Happy the Heart

The heart that prays will rise up comforted.
The heart that serves the Lord is filled with joy.
In all his days, he shall have meat and bread;
His faith is one that nothing shall destroy.

A heart made strong by loving, unseen Power,
That reads and cherishes the Holy Word,
Shall see fulfillment in each coming hour.
Happy the heart that waits upon the Lord!

How to Pray Effectively

"After this manner therefore pray ye ... "
Matthew 6:9

People frequently ask the question: How does one pray effectively? Jesus in His Sermon on the Mount said; "When thou prayest, enter into thy closet, and when thou hast shut thy door, pray to thy Father which is in secret; and thy Father which seeth in secret shall reward thee openly." Matthew 6:6.

By turning directly to God in prayer for all our needs and for the answers to the difficult problems which we face, we will receive help and guidance from above to do what is right. We must affirm the totality and the power of God, The Holy Spirit. We must come to Him with faith in His goodness and power, knowing that He answers every proper prayer, but that He answers in His own way and in His own time. We must come to Him on bended knee and with humility in our hearts.

Through our prayers, we come closer to God and to

His holy Son. Prayer makes us open and receptive to the good that God has already prepared for us. "Before they call I will answer." God is the answer, and He will answer the need of every one of His children. Each of us must learn how to pray. Prayer is the way in which we are able to open the channel for God's power and will to work through us.

The prayers of God's people are the means by which He carries on His great work on earth. Prayer opens a limitless storehouse. God's hands withhold nothing from the prayers made in faith. The greatest and mightiest of successes that come are created and carried on by prayer.

God's house on earth is a house of prayer. His earthly armies are clothed with the spoils of victory and His enemies are defeated on every hand. God gives the reassurance that there is good in all things. When something happens that seems contrary to this, it is because we see only with limited vision, not realizing that His goodness unfolds in ways which we may not always be able to perceive or comprehend. We must never let go of our faith and trust in God, nor let it grow dim or weak. Although we may at times feel far from God, we must always remember that we are not separated from Him.

It has been said that we grow in the direction of our eyes; that what we fix our eyes upon, our attention toward, will largely determine what our lives will be. The familiar expression, "When the outlook is not good, try the uplook," is most apropos in these dark, troubled times, which demand all the courage, both physical and moral, that we can summon. Our foes are not only those of flesh and blood, but, in addition, we must often wrestle with the problems and temptations of evil. Christ says, "In the world ye shall have tribulation," but He adds his marvelous reassurance, "Be of good cheer; I have overcome the world." John 16:33.

When we turn to God in prayer, all the spiritual resources of the universe are called into action to work out the right answer, the perfect answer to our individual needs. But we need to cleanse our minds and block out all negative thinking, all limited belief, all doubts and fears. We must come to God with the feeling that we are His children and know that He loves us with a love that is beyond human understanding.

_ Prayer involves a change of thought, a reorientation of the mind from the negative forebodings that any difficult problem may present, to the positive awareness of God's understanding presence.

It is not difficult to pray when we go apart to talk with God, when we shut the door of our minds to material things and open the windows of our souls to heaven. What makes prayer difficult is that the things of the world act as static on the line of communication from our souls to heaven.

Paul indicated very clearly in his letter to the Ephesians that God is much closer than most people will believe. "In whom we have boldness and access with confidence by the faith of him." Ephesians 3:12. To many with little faith, God seems very far away because they are looking for Him in the wrong place and for the wrong reason.

God is faithful, and His word and promise are sure and certain. He is just and He is merciful. Confession unburdens our hearts and prepares us to receive God's grace and mercy through the channel of prayer. God has come to us in Christ and made Himself known to us. The Resurrection of our Lord from His death on the cross brought victory over death. And His ascension into heaven shows that the way to God has been reopened.

Prayer is an act of worship through which we make known our requests before God and offer our praise and thanksgiving for His many blessings. It develops a spirit of nearness to God and a greater concern for our fellowman. In prayer, we should ask for things which glorify God and also things which are to our own and our neighbor's welfare. When praying for spiritual blessings we can ask unconditionally; when praying for other gifts, we must ask that God grant them according to His will, in His own way and at His own time.

Prayer is a spiritual experience, in which we are lifted from low ideals to high ideals, from vulgarity and callousness and selfishness to a finer quality of life; from hate and malice and misunderstanding to a spirit of warm love and Christian brotherhood.

In prayer, we have a desire to walk in the light of truth, to lift the horizons of our minds and spirits, to seek and strive for nobler ideals of living, and to love our neighbors as ourselves. Humility is the first step in true prayer. One can pray anywhere and at any time. The spirit of meekness and humility is essential in that it unlocks the door to God's presence. The opening of the soul toward God is a wholesome experience.

The right attitude in prayer is to realize that the divine will for man is all good, and that we must accept God's will completely. "Thy will be done" is a phrase that should be uppermost in our minds when we pray. God's wisdom and knowledge are infinitely greater than ours. He will send to us only those things which He knows are best for our good.

A Moment's Prayer

When men will pause awhile and stand and listen,
When heads are bowed, hands folded, and with heart
Attuned to catch the faintest whisper heard,
Then each will find that he and God are not apart.

The holiness within that pause for reverence
Will still the world's wild clamor, din will cease,
And hearts will find a strength for greater labor,
Now fortified with quiet, inner peace.

A moment's prayer! It stills the greatest longing
To go a devious way. It calms all fear.
It makes each heart rejoice, for it will bless
And bring the knowledge that our Lord is near.

Prayer

Prayer should not be vain petition,
Not a bargaining with God,
Never just a conversation
But a rest from roads we trod.

Prayer is faith and adoration.
Prayer's a song of love and praise.
Prayer's a hymn for one who worships.
Prayer's the strength of all our days.

Remember to Pray

Begin your every day with God.
    Repeat a little prayer
And thank Him for the coming day
    And for His blessed care.

And open wide the Book of God
    And read a verse or two
And ask that His great love and grace
    Always remain with you.

If you will only lift your heart
    And seek His love to share,
His radiance will flood your soul.
    We're near to God in prayer.

Food for the Hungry

Now there is rich abundance
Of luscious orchard fruit,
The product of the rain and sun
And tree and branch and root.

And fields of waving beauty,
The wheat for making bread;
Thank God for full-sheaved harvest.
A world waits to be fed.

The Heart that Prays

Heart, do not be impatient,
But learn this vital thing:
Most surely, God will answer
Each prayer you pray or sing.

The heart that prays will surely
Be fed and comforted—
His living water quenches thirst,
His body is our bread.

Kneel Down in Prayer!

O come, let us bow down and worship Him!
He is our Shepherd; sheep of His dear hand
Are we, the people of His golden pasture,
Most wonderful of all His wondrous land.
Renew your strength by kneeling down to Him.

Lift up your heart, but humbly bow your head.
A prayer will take away your doubt and fear.
Get down on knees—there is no better way
For you to find that God is very near.
Assured you now will know the path to tread.

Prayers

Prayer must come from humble hearts
    Our pleas to Him proclaim
Our faith, our hope, our love for Him
    Are spoken in His name.

Prayers that come from believing hearts
    Are open to His love
And every prayer is subject to
    The will of God above.

The Joy of Meditation

"... His delight is in the law of the Lord;
and in his law doth he meditate day and night."
                                                    Psalm 1:2

Men have always felt the need of help from a power greater than themselves. The answer to every problem facing mankind today can be found in prayer, in spiritual communion with God.

By lifting our thoughts above the material to the spiritual, and by shutting out the noisy and demanding claims of the physical senses that life is material and discordant, we can realize the presence of God.

In meditation, we must be very patient in our endeavor to conquer any sense of unrest. Truth comes from within, and the truth revealed by our own consciousness becomes the "light of the world."

In meditation, we attain a sense of peace and

harmony, and a realization of the presence of Christ. But one of the greatest hindrances to meditation is the fear that we do not have enough understanding with which to begin the practice.

There can be no limit to understanding if our dependence is on God's and not our own. It is the great understanding of God which is important, not ours. In quietness and confidence, let us turn within, to let truth reveal itself to us. Like the Psalmist, in the 147th Psalm, let us dispose of any fears and doubts by believing "Great is our Lord, and of great power: his understanding is infinite."

Our Lord spent much of His time in silent meditation and communion. We may be very certain that He was not asking the Father for anything for Himself or of a material nature. Actually, we may assume that He was not asking for anything; He was listening—for God's direction and God's instruction, guidance, and support.

Most people have never learned how to sit down by themselves, be quiet and contemplative. Many have never learned how to be quiet enough to read a book. They want entertainment, and settle for watching the television programs, seeing with their eyes, hearing with their ears, but giving their minds complete rest.

The object in meditation is to attain quietness and receptivity, but not to completely blank out the mind. Actually, one cannot really blot out the mind, for our brain is an active piece of machinery, running full-blast at all times. But a period of peacefulness and quietness will allow the mind to slow down considerably, with the result that extraneous thoughts will gradually disappear.

When we feel a desire to meditate and find that our mind is in a turmoil, a state of confusion, with our thoughts running in helter-skelter fashion, we should not attempt to blank the mind completely or to blot out all the disturbing thoughts. Instead, relax as much as possible, and turn to the Scriptures and read quietly for awhile.

"Be still and know that I am God" is a good thought for us to remember, for it will bring peacefulness and calm within us. A calm and serene mind is the prerequisite for hearing the still, small voice. Quiet meditation is a powerful and potent medicine.

In meditation, there is an area of consciousness revealed through which we can be instantly one with God. Keeping the mind stayed on God leads to a greater awareness of Him. The activity of Christ is by no means limited to the past, when He actually lived on earth. We can experience Christ today as did those people who lived in His day. This awareness is the beginning of a life of grace. "Acquaint now thyself with Him and be at peace."

"Peace be still" will become the master of every storm of our existence. The presence of Christ will go before us, to help us along the rugged places and to make our way light. We will live "not by might nor by power, but by my Spirit."

The Scriptures tell us in I Corinthians 2:14 that the natural man does not understand the gifts of God. We must understand that when we come to God in all humility with our prayers, it is not actually we who are praying but the Spirit of God meditating within us. We simply open our consciousness to let this Spirit reveal to us our need and to furnish us its fulfillment.

In prayer and meditation, our attitude should be: "Speak, Lord; for thy servant heareth." I Samuel 3:9

Man Must Walk with Calmness

There is a strong and steadfast, loving Power
That rules each sunlit day, each starlit night.
It guides the brilliant sun upon its way,
The silvery moon in its celestial flight.

Its equilibrium is all its own.
The Power calms the tides that ebb and flow,
It knows the destiny of every thing
And tells each season when to come and go.

And man, the tiniest in nature's plan,
Must know His steadfast ways; and let the clear,
Calm inner voice speak out and still his ways
So he may walk with calmness through each year.

A Quiet Hour with Jesus

A quiet hour with Jesus
    Will bring unfailing grace,
For being in His presence,
    You're in a holy place.
But worldly cares and problems
    Must all be left outside;
Give Him your undivided heart;
    In Him you must confide.

You'll gain new strength and courage
    Within this quiet hour,
Your faith and trust grow stronger
    With all His love and power.
You'll gain a keener vision,
    To see things clearer still
And have desire to bear His cross,
    To do the Master's will.

A quiet hour with Jesus
    Is one you must hold dear,
For under His protecting wings
    There is no doubt, no fear.
When our lives are one with Him
    Then let our hearts proclaim
That we will always follow Him
    For service in His name.

Meditation of the Heart

If we devote more time to purer thought,
And if illumination we do seek,
Then the effort we make to understand
Can bring new strength when all ahead seems bleak.

We each must find the way that meets our need
For understanding and for peace of mind.
There are many paths that we can follow,
Our answer from above we each must find.

We all can pray, and every prayer will lead us
To realms of rightness and of great release.
God's ever-active Spirit in our being
Will bring us harmony and joy and peace.

Answered Prayer

When worries seem too much for me,
When trials are hard to bear,
I find it well to stop awhile
And bow my head in prayer.

I tell God of my need of Him,
He puts my world aright.
I rise and take my load again,
My burden now is light.

The Lord's Shelter

I dare not trust a shelter built by man
In which to hide, but gladly would I share
The shelter which the love of God provides,
The God who keeps us in His precious care.

I find the shelter built beneath His wings
Has room for all. Each one may find a place;
May find the radiant joy and happiness
Which grow from His great love and tender grace.

And so I pray, O Lord, to be with Thee
When earthly life for me shall gently cease.
Look down with mercy; lead me by Thy hand
Into the blessed shelter of Thy peace.

Aloneness

I am not one who would disdain
A place where man can be alone,
Though happiness is found with those
Whose friendship we have always known.

But I am breathless with the wonder
That may be found in solitude;
Man needs a time for meditation,
Where soul and spirit are renewed.

Things of Peace

A pleasing peace is found in common things.
    Serenity will gently emanate
From tranquil maples growing by the lane
    Or from the lilacs blooming by the gate.

With pews worn smooth by years of constant use,
    A small church in a quiet country place
Will know the essence of tranquillity,
    Will be imbued with an enduring grace.

The reverent beauty of a lovely song
    Will cause upsetting discord to depart.
The stillness of the bright and shining stars
    Will bring true peace to any weary heart.

From the pale moon which spreads her silver light
    Upon the world, a benediction flows;
And from the evening song of whippoorwills
    A peace will come as dusk to darkness grows.

In a Quiet Hour

Within the quiet of an hour
Where we with God can be alone,
The heart will find a greater power
To walk the pathway to His throne.

One finds a comfort, strength, and balm,
Surcease from selfishness and greed,
For such a peacefulness and calm
Supplies a deep and vital need.

Where Beauty Dwells

Where quiet hills and solemn valleys sleep,
Where calm and peaceful prairies are not stirred
And changing splendors of the day are seen,
The rhythmic heartbeat of the world is heard.

Here, there is time and space and room to grow.
Here, one may find the secret of release.
Here, silence is transmuted into song
And hearts may find hushed beauty, gentle peace.

Here, dreams may live—too beautiful for words.
Here, we may walk with God, and proudly see
The grail of wonder, reaching for the stars.
Here, soul can rest in true tranquillity.

Night's Healing Power

There is healing in harvest fields at dusk,
When shadows lengthen and the air grows still
And quietness has come. The peacefulness
Which settles down is by the Master's will.

Man's work is done and all man's noise and din
Have died away and nature's sounds take over:
The little rippling winds, the crickets' chirp,
A lark's late song,—each is a peaceful cover.

The tired horses neigh within their stalls,
Feeling a gratefulness for blessed rest,
And glowing windows bring a needed strength
To tired harvester, new life and zest.

Night brings a calm. The essences of life
Must be renewed—in man, in beast, in earth.
God planned it so. And by this miracle,
He gives to each a kindly healing worth.

The Need of Expectancy

... Look for new heavens and a new earth."
II Peter 3: 13

Christianity should be a religion of expectancy. Today, religion all too often seems a dull thing. The radiance of the early Church was lost when it lost its expectancy. This must be restored.

Christianity is a most powerful factor in our society, for it is the pillar of our institutions. It regulates the family, enjoins private and public virtues, and builds moral character. It teaches us to love God supremely and to love our neighbor as ourself. It makes good men and useful citizens. It encourages every virtue and denounces every vice; it promotes and serves the public welfare; it upholds peace and order.

He who is lacking in a love of human kindness, is lacking in a love for God. We live today in troublesome times. Fears, doubts, endless worries and sorrows seem to beset us. We lose heart. We become discouraged. Our faith grows dim and weak. But such experiences are not new to mankind. If we, like David in I Samuel 30, will rely on the eternal God, we can also sing with him that the Lord is our rock, and our fortress, and our deliverer. If God be for us, who can be against us?

Less human expectations and more divine ones will make our lives more Christlike, and will be the secret of a full and abundant life. The measure of our lives is found in the reach and source of our expectation. David, in Psalm 62:5, states: "My soul, wait thou only upon God; for my expectation is from him."

Many persons, lacking an expectancy of an eternal life, are filled more with an expectancy of what is to happen today—or tomorrow. But God's Word, in Proverbs 27:1, informs us to: "Boast not thyself of tomorrow; for thou knowest not what a day may bring forth."

In James 4:14, God says: "Whereas ye know not what shall be on the morrow. For what is your life? It is even a vapour, that appeareth for a little time, and then vanisheth away."

Each of us who are followers of Christ must keep moving forward and carry our portion of the Cross of Jesus. God will never ask us to bear more than we are able to carry. Often in our weakness of faith, we may think that God has permitted us to carry an unbearable cross. We may be tempted to accuse God of being too harsh with us when we have our trials of tragedy, economic failure, crippling accidents, or when illness strikes. But the believer in Christ should know from God's Word that the Lord never burdens one of His children with a cross he cannot carry. God alone knows our limit of endurance.

But rest assured, God will either remove your cross or will grant you the power to carry it. Whatever comes, it will be because of His will; let us believe that God's will is always good and gracious, even though we may not be able to understand it at all times.

Let us rejoice that the Spirit of Christ within us ever urges us onward and upward. We should have no greater joy than to know that we are growing, improving, progressing. Growth in life means growth in health, vitality, strength; it means growth in wisdom and understanding; it means growth in capability and the power to accomplish even more. God is the substance out of which every good thing comes. Knowing that God's abundance is forever surrounding and supplying us, our assurance should be complete. "My God shall supply all your need according to his riches in glory by Christ Jesus." Philippians 4:19. "And we know that all things work together for good to them that love God." Romans 8:28.

Expectancy is a form of prayer, a contemplation of God in and through all. We gain an understanding of our oneness with God when we recognize the divine Presence in ourselves, and let it express all that we think, see, say, or do.

Meditation will provide the channel for divine ideas to flow in. "Be still, and know that I am God," we are told in Psalm 46:10. And as we do this, becoming fully aware of God's holy presence in us and surrounding us, we will open ourselves to His truth. Freed from a sense of limitation, God's wisdom will speak to us, will reveal itself, will cooperate with us, guiding and directing us in His pathway. We will walk in light.

"Know ye not that ye are the temple of God, and that the Spirit of God dwelleth in you?" I Corinthians 3:16.

By letting God's divine Holy Spirit rule us, we increase our vessel of abundance and receive a greater measure of good. We will come to an awareness that the more light we use, the more will be given us. There is an abundant supply always at our command, if we have the faith, and the expectancy necessary to obtain them.

Success in anything begins first in the mind. The fulfillment of our dream will depend upon our envisioning the right ideas and accepting them, working with them to achieve success. Inspiration often gives us the right ideas, but inspiration must still be translated into action to accomplish our goal.

Inspiration, coupled with faith and complete confidence in the knowledge that our efforts are being properly channelled, will lead to success and happiness. When we expect the best and work actively toward achieving the best, we will receive the best.

Matthew 17:20 tells us: "If ye have faith as a grain of mustard seed ... nothing shall be impossible unto you."

True happiness is experiencing presence of God's Holy Spirit within our beings. We are realizing our potential for good. We are alive with a harmonious spirit of the indwelling Presence, and only good can come from our great expectancy.

Interlude

Winter has come and summer is over,
Summer is gone and the bins are filled;
The fields lie sere and bare; the clover,
Withered and dead, and all is stilled.

The plow lies rusting—a useless thing.
Root and seed and leaf must sleep
Until earth turns again to Spring
And life once more shall thrive and leap.

Compassion

"Suffering with another" is one way
Compassion is defined. It brings relief
And helps to ease the pain of one who may
Have lost his faith, his trust, in time of grief.

Compassion is the same this modern day
As when our Lord walked, on Galilee's shore,
Showing His love to those along His way
He comforts us now and for evermore.

Contrition

When someone was in need of me,
    I did not heed,
Unknowing that I soon would be
    Also in need.

Someone reached out his helping hand
    And someone shared.
Thank God someone could understand,
    That someone cared!

We Who Would Receive

I know that prayer is answered.
My heart is not amazed
At any of God's blessings.
Our God is to be praised.

I know God's loving mercy
And all His love for me,
His graciousness and kindness,
His generosity.

Seeing that His bounteous gifts
Are everywhere around
We must be humbly thankful
God's treasures still abound.

Small Minds

The one who is content to rest
    Upon some minor victory won,
Shall never see the splendid crest
    Nor see the rise of blazing sun.

Content to dwell in lowly places
    And make his home in valleys deep,
He'll miss the splendor of high spaces
    And the blessings of his God to reap.

Preparedness

A cup of tea, a piece of bread,—
With these my body will be fed;
But other things are needed still
To do God's work, to do His will.

A patient heart, the will to work,
Strong, willing hands that will not shirk
Appointed tasks, a mind that's wise
Enough to teach, far-seeing eyes.

With these possessions, and my soul
God gives me strength to seek my goal,
And try to do the work that He,
Expectantly, has given me.

Evidence

The scoffers scoff, the scorners scorn,
    The unbelievers doubt,
For each must have a miracle
    To put their ways to rout.

But in the glory of a rose
    That grows from miry sod,
By touch of sun and kiss of rain,
    Is proof enough of God.

Around God's Throne

The angel hosts around God's throne
Shall welcome each new pilgrim soul,
Shall clothe him in the whitest robe;
He shall be cleansed, made pure and whole.

His days shall be a wondrous glory
And there shall be no pain-filled night;
His life shall be an endless story
Of grace and love, of great delight.

The Tonic of Joy

"... Joy cometh in the morning."
Psalm 30:5

The Christian religion is a religion of joy, and all Christians are to be messengers of joy, witnesses of the Resurrection. Jesus tells us: "I will see you again, and your heart shall rejoice, and your joy no man taketh from you." John 16:22. "Ask, and ye shall receive, that your joy may be full." John 16:24.

Our hearts should be filled with Christian joy. In John 15:11, Christ tells us: "These things have I spoken unto you, that my joy might remain in you, and that your joy might be full," and again in John 16:20, "Your sorrow shall be turned to joy."

A Christian should be a happy person. He should learn the full meaning of joyousness in his heart, for this eternal life. Now is the accepted time of salvation and joy.

Christian joy is not an easy contentment, and can never be a naive self-satisfaction with things as they are. The place we give to joy and happiness is the place that we give to God.

Joy should be the keynote of our lives; joy in the confidence that God is, was, and ever shall be, and that we are here only because of Him. Joy should reign in our lives because we are His people and are called to serve Him.

Each one of us will discover that love is a way of life, and with it comes great joy. The more that love is given, the more joy it will return. Joy is born in human hearts and brings spiritual peace.

If we remember the greatest truth that "God is love," other thoughts will fit into a pattern that is nearer to perfection because this simple statement will answer many of life's perplexing problems.

Love is a warmth felt within that radiates joy and shines forth to light not only our own lives but the lives of many others with whom we come in contact.

Like the Psalmist David, we should "serve the Lord with gladness." Psalm 100:2. We must serve God with all our heart, with all our mind, and with all our soul, serving Him with gladness. God's children are joyful when their hearts are in the service of giving. It is within the power of each of us to be a blessing, and to have joy that knows no limit if we, at our journey's end, can say, with Paul: "I have kept the faith." II Timothy 4:7.

Proverbs 17:22 tells us: "A merry heart doeth good like a medicine." A cheerful heart can be cultivated.

We must learn to have faith in God and to accept Him and the good which He offers. It is a joyous thing to trust in the goodness of God.

Joy is a quality of life which transcends pleasure. Genuine joy has to do with one's spirit, one's inner being. Joy is the cadence which brings the music of harmony into our lives. Our source of joy is to be caught up in a purpose so much greater than our own that we may be freed from selfishness and self-centeredness. When we know Christ, we will show more kindness to others. God is a God of love, and when we become His children, we will have love in our hearts and joy in abundance.

In the Bible, the word "joy" is found twice as often as the word "sorrow." "The fruit of the Spirit is ... joy ... " Galatians 5:22. "The joy of the Lord is your strength." Nehemiah 8:10. "The kingdom of God is ... joy in the Holy Ghost." Romans 14:17. "I will joy in the God of my salvation." Habakkuk 3:18. " ... Your joy no man taketh from you." John 16:22. "Now the God of hope fill you with all joy and peace in believing, that ye may abound in hope, through the power of the Holy Ghost." Romans 15:13.

When God revealed Himself to the world, He filled the world with joy. He came to us as a little babe, pure and sweet and innocent, wanting our love. He stretched His little hands to us, in love, confidence, and innocence. How many of us reached forth to the Child, in love, with yearning, with compassion, with eagerness, filled with joy?

Joyful Hearts

When hearts are glad,
It is a way of praying.
I'm sure God knows
It is a way of saying
Our thanks to Him
For all that we receive.
When hearts are glad,
It shows that we believe.

Our Saviour's Birth

There is a song of praise and worship
That fills each heart at Christmastime.
It tells of love beyond our telling;
It tells of love that is sublime.

The shepherds were the first to hear it,
This song, in far-off Eastern skies.
Now, every land has heard the message
Of this great song that never dies.

A composition of the angels,
Its harmony is sweet and strong.
It echoes on through all the ages—
A glorious, triumphant song.

Keepsake

A heart should have the strength of will,
    Discarding recklessly
The cares and woes of grief and pain,
    The things that should not be.

A heart should only want to keep
    The really lasting thing,
The radiant and glorious
    That causes heart to sing.

Joy

Joy shall be the glory of our days.
Joy shall bring a peace to mind and heart.
Joy shall come in unknown myriad ways
And bring a gladness that shall not depart.

Joy must be the keynote of each life,
The rapture that shall conquer grief and sorrow;
Joy shall calm the chaos, still the strife,
And be the substance of each bright tomorrow.

Pot of Gold

To you, who think the rainbow's end
Is in some distant, far-off place,
You've never seen emotions blend
In some small child's enraptured face,
Receiving an undreamed-of gift.
Nor have you heard the warbled notes
Of liquid melodies which lift
A tired soul, from songbirds' throats.

Nor have you seen wild plums in bloom,
Whose boughs of petalled foam, flame-bright,
Cascaded beauty and perfume;
A mountain's stark and sunlit height;
The white waves breaking on a shore;
Nor heard love's story, often told.
These things—and many, many more—
Can be a rainbow's pot of gold.

Happiness

Happiness
Can be your own today
If you, with heart and lips,
Will speak words you should say.

Happiness
Will come and stay awhile
If you can only teach
Another's heart to smile.

Happiness
Will come and not be brief
If you, by friendliness,
Can ease another's grief.

Happiness—
You have the right to live it
If you, by word and deed,
Will try your best go give it.

Joy Blooms

If beautiful blossoms always grow
Within the garden of your mind,
And if, each day, you plant new seed,
You should not be surprised to find
The seasons will be fruitful ones;
And banish sorrows, doubts, and fears;
The lilt of laughter, happiness,
And friendship last through all the years.

May Each Have Faith

May each have faith!
Let there be shining gladness
In all the tasks
Awaiting us to do.
May each have faith
Although there may be sadness
And pain for us
Before our task is through.

May each have faith!
Let hearts be true and strong;
May each one know
Tomorrow he will find,
Behind the grief and pain,
A joyous song;
Will find God's peace,
The dream of all mankind.

Shining Your Light

"The Lord is my light and my salvation;
whom shall I fear?"

Psalm 27:1

Jesus said: "I am the light of the world: he that
followeth me shall not walk in darkness, but shall
have the light of life." John 8:12.

It is only through our love for Jesus and our
following His way that we are able to shine our light.
When He comes into our hearts, ours will be a radiant
light and ours will be a joyous song. If we are willing
to let our light shine, God will put it where it can be
seen to the best advantage and where it will do the
most good. Only as we can reflect our love for Jesus,
can we send forth a light that may lead others to Him.

The joy and spiritual warmth that we may reflect
come from the inward grace and knowledge of

knowing His love, so that we become lights for His glory.

We are told in Matthew 5:14 that "Ye are the light of the world," and in verse 16, "Let your light so shine before men, that they may see your good works, and glorify your Father which is in heaven." In Luke 11:35, we are told: "Take heed therefore that the light which is in thee be not darkness."

Our work is to lead others into Christ's kingdom of love and light. True Christian living is living for others. Our Lord Jesus offers comfort and consolation to all who will listen to His voice. Through faith in God and in fellowship with Christ's followers, we will find solace and peace of mind, a fuller understanding of the needs of every human being. A Christian's duty is to be a helping friend.

Psalm 133:1 tells us: "Behold, how good and pleasant it is for brethren to dwell in unity!" And Ephesians 2:14 informs us: "He is our peace, who hath made both one, and hath broken down the middle wall of partition between us."

If our journey through life is to be from darkness to light, what will be our light? There may be times when we will not be able to see clearly because of the darkness in our own lives. Our life is God's life; let us live it for Him.

Jesus tells us in John 12:46: "I am come a light into the world, that whosoever believeth on me should not abide in darkness."

The need for vision, for spiritual enlightenment, is an ever-constant need. This need can only be met by turning to Jesus the source of light. As we seek the light found in Christ through prayer, we will find its radiance shining within us. This Christ-radiance can make one truly a child of God.

We will thus be transformed by the renewing of our minds. Our lights will shine. We will become alive, warmed by God's love and mercy. The immensity of our influence will be beyond our imaging.

When we will let go of the past and accept with faith the things that are of God, then will the way be opened for new blessings to come into our lives. We will become new creatures, confident, happy, courageous, filled with love and power. God will have dominion over us and will guide our lives along His pathway.

Walking in Light

God's light dispels the power of the darkness
For darkness hides the goal, the journey's way.
The vision that He gives will light our footpath
And guide our feet aright and not astray.

And we believers will march on in triumph,
Our faith undimmed and walking in God's light,
Our vision growing as we leave the darkness
And see the splendor of the star-tipped height.

Mine the Common Task

My lot is cast with lowly ones. I shared
Their meagerness on earth and never cared
That glamour was not mine. The simple thing
Is still enough for me. My heart shall sing
When life's brief day is past and I must go
To my appointed place. Full well, I know
I shall be satisfied and only ask
That I may do my simple humble task.

Where Heaven Is

Heaven is never very far,
It's not a distant land;
Heaven can be within your heart,
A gift within your hand.

If you are kind and merciful,
Compassionate, and strong
In doing work that should be done,
And help to right a wrong;

If you give heed to one in pain
Or help to one in need,
Be generous with scanty fare
Without a thought of greed;

If you can take the common task
And do the greater part,—
Then heaven's very close to you,
It lives within your heart.

Capabilities

You can light a little candle
Which will help to clear the dark;
You can speak a word of courage
To someone who needs this spark
To begin a rugged journey,
Help begin his upward climb;
You can breathe a silent prayer
Which may help a worried mind.

You can sing a song of gladness
Which may help someone to sing;
You can spread a little sunshine
By your helpfulness, and bring
Happiness and cheerful thinking
To someone now sick with pain;
By your friendliness and courage,
Help a scared one smile again.

Light of Living Truth

There is a light for every darkened day,
There is a living truth which we may see,
Though grief at times may make us very blind
We cannot see it. There shall always be
A guilding light, a living truth. Each soul
And each believing heart must learn to find
The tall white taper which will light his way,
The living truth to make him free and whole.

Brighteners

A lighted candle in the dark
    Can bring a bit of day,
Its radiant and shining spark
    Will chase the dark away.

A friendly word, a cheerful smile
    Will chase away the gloom
From someone's weary heart awhile
    And cause a joy to bloom.

Bear Grief with Silence

When grief must come, I find that I must go
To be alone with pain that none should share.
The treasured joys and happiness I know
Are only known to those for whom I care.

The ones I love can only share my mirth;
From them I shield my grief and pain and sorrow.
I hold their friendship of far greater worth,
And hope that it will grow with each tomorrow.

Sharing

May I bring to some sad and lonely friend
A touch of friendliness and cheerfulness;
A joyful radiance, which I may lend,
Made up of courage and of fearlessness.

If God has placed into my hands for sharing
Great treasure from His bounty, may I be
The more distributor, to ease despairing
And add to hope and faith both joy and glee.

Tomorrow

The one who thinks tomorrow lies
    Within his selfish hand,
Whose mind has great complacency
    And cannot understand
Tomorrow is for those who share
    Today, its joy and sorrow;
The heart that knows but selfishness
    Will have no glad tomorrow.

The heart must know a kindliness,
    The brotherhood of man;
Must know responsibility
    And do the best it can
To bring a peace to every soul,
    A joy to every life,
Or else that heart will feel the pain
    Of sorrow, grief, and strife.

Faith in Action

"... thy faith hath made thee whole."
Luke 17:19

Faith in action becomes a tremendous force for good. It requires that we look at life positively. True faith builds inner strength and removes obstacles from our pathway. Faith in action is well described in the second chapter of James which summarizes this principle: "This is how it is with faith: if it is alone and has no actions with it, then it is dead." James 2:17 (T.E.V.)

While faith is intensely personal, it is something which must be shared. A strong and active faith makes itself known to others. If faith lives in the heart, it will shine forth in our lives. When we have a strong faith, and as we put our faith into action, we are able, through the working of the Holy Spirit, to meet all challenges victoriously. This is well demonstrated

when the apostle Paul compliments the Christians at
Thessalonica for their faith: "For we remember before
our God and Father how you put your faith into
practice, how your love made you work so hard, and
how your hope in our Lord Jesus Christ is firm."
I Thessalonians 1:3 (T.E.V.) "You became an example
to all believers." I Thessalonians 1:7 (T.E.V.)

A great faith will never permit us to evade the task
at hand. Only those who have given their hearts to
God and who give themselves wholeheartedly to do
that which is good and needful in the sight of God can
truly offer all of their resources for Him.

Faith in action brings assurance, and assurance
results in confidence. Confidence, joined with the
divine forces of God's Holy Spirit that is at our
disposal, results in the ability to produce a miracle of
accomplishment. The Holy Scriptures tell us that a
faith the size of a mustard seed will be able to move
a mountain. We can have faith in God because He is
always faithful to us.

Everyone needs the solid dependability of faith in
God. While we have a dependency on, and confidence
in, our fellowman, we also frequently have a
subconscious knowledge that we must allow for his
shortcomings, because of man's imperfection. There is
no person whom we know who will always come up
to our expectations. Oftentimes this may cause us
dismay, sometimes even despair. On occasion, we may
even doubt ourselves. But God will never fail us.

A truly dedicated Christian will not change with the
changing times, when it comes to spiritual matters.

God's Word does not change, as Psalm 119:89 informs us, and when we are following God's Word, nothing must deter us from our path. We must remain steadfast in our thinking and in our faith and permit nothing to stop us from serving the Lord. This is really faith in action.

As Christians, we must never turn aside from God's purpose and will, to follow any allurements of this world. We must not—we cannot— divide our allegiance and loyalty to Christ. We must serve either God or worldly wealth and pleasure; we cannot serve both.

Faith and repentance are tremendous words in the Bible. Through them, we are saved and joined to Christ; we accept Him in our hearts and develop a willingness to serve Him. We must never lose our spiritual wisdom and vision.

We are joined together in a common faith, as explained in Acts 11:17-18, and as ambassadors for Christ, we must maintain the teachings of Holy Scripture and our principles, or we lose our unity and our message. If we lose sight of the purpose of the gospel we preach, we will have no peace or hope in this troubled world.

A dedicated Christian is not afraid to speak of his love for his Saviour before men. He is ever ready, ever able, and willing to tell of the love he has in his heart and of his commitment to Christ. He has no other goal but to serve the Lord to the best of his ability.

The teachings of man must be judged by the teachings of God. Man's folly is his attempt to bend his thinking to fit his own purpose, when the Holy

Scriptures teach that man must conform to the teachings of God's Word.

A personal faith in God and in His Holy Son Jesus Christ means that we will serve Him and none other. We willingly choose Him, accept Him, believe in Him, and in love dedicate our lives to Him. It is only in this way that we can put our faith into action.

We will never be able to build a brotherhood by means of hatred, prejudice or destruction. But there is no possible doubt that if the principles for living laid down by Jesus Christ were followed to the letter by everyone, the nations of the world could live together in peace, harmony and prosperity.

Christ's way is practical, not just idealistic. It is a commonsense way of life. Deep Christian convictions will always lead to a higher plane of living. When Christ is in our hearts, we will always be right in our thinking and action. Christ makes it possible for us to always walk in His way.

Faith in action—walking the way of Christ—brings joy and peace to the heart.

Role of the Faithful

I know that I must walk aright
With faith and very tall,
That I must bravely face and fight
When sin or evil call.

I know that I must never sleep
While He, the Master, prays,
But wait, wide-eyed, and ever keep
The spirit of His ways.

And though I see hate's cruel face,
The javelins of scorn,
Yet ever will I seek my place
Beside the Highest Born.

Your Mind

Make of your mind
A palace, fine and clean,
Where good thoughts live,
Alert and bright and keen;
Lit with the splendor
Of a righteous heart,
Where sin and evilness
Will have no part.

God's Stars

No other gladness stirs the heart
As that which comes to us afar,
Beyond the pale, dim glow of space—
The silver wonder of a star.

A star is beautiful and bright,
Steadfast, unfailing, stilled with peace.
It spreads a comfort, restfulness,
And certainty that shall not cease.

God calls each one by name; not one
Has ever failed nor light grown dim.
Lift up your eyes and see their light
And then feel very close to Him!

The Lord's Promise

We cannot bring Him down to us,
    He lifts us up to Him.
And though we bleed from thorn and flint,
    We still can sing a hymn
Of love and praise, of thankfulness
    For all His love and care,
For if He did not show His love,
    Our hearts would know despair.

A living promise He has made
    To every follower.
Where He goes, we may also go
    And find great comfort there.
"Come unto Me, I'll give you rest,"
    I hear the Saviour plead.
And I believe His spoken words
    And go where He will lead.

Assistants to God

God has no other hands but ours
    To do His work for Him
And if we love God as we should,
    We'll labor on with Him.

God has no other feet but ours
    To lead men to His way,
So we should walk along with Him,
    Help others in dismay.

God has no other tongues but ours
    To tell of all His love,
So we should always speak of Him
    And His great home above.

The Resurrection Story

The story of our Lord's great Resurrection
Brings joy and peace to every knowing heart.
The message of the triumph of the ages
Is heard in lonely place and crowded mart.

Each Easter means to followers of Christ
The regal crowning of the passing year,
And every faithful one takes up His cross
Without regret, without a doubt or fear.

Each one shall see the Saviour's gentle face
And each shall hear His kind and gentle voice;
Each sings His praise in love and reverence;
Each happy heart knows joy and shall rejoice.

The anthem tells its glorious joyful story
In pealing tones of melody and cheer;
The stone of dread is rolled away forever
From every heart that willingly will hear.

The Spirit of Gratitude

"O give thanks unto the Lord."
Psalm 105:1

Gratitude is one of the most beautiful flowers that bloom in the heart. Gratitude is a rare and precious thing. When our hearts are grateful, we give our thanks of appreciation. When we are truly thankful to God for His wonderful blessings, He will pour even more of them upon us.

We praise the Lord with our lips and by the testimony of our lives. Usually, actions will speak louder than words. Daily we receive so many good things from the hand of God that we have abundant reason to express our gratitude to Him.

"It is a good thing to give thanks unto the Lord, and to sing praises unto thy name, O most High: to show forth thy lovingkindness in the morning, and thy faithfulness every night." Psalm 92:1-2.

There is no more genuine satisfaction than that which comes to us from diligent practice of Christian benevolence. The Lord has promised in grace to reward the faithful deeds of love performed by His children. God's children should consider it a glorious privilege to assist others who are less fortunate. Christians cannot remain indifferent to the needs of others. A living faith is active in good works.

The ancient words of invitation, "Let us give thanks unto the Lord our God," call for a response from us. God has been good to us, and our hearts should overflow with thanksgiving. Every Christian should reecho the words of the prophet Zechariah when he acclaims: "How great is His goodness." Zechariah 9:17. Good things will always happen to us when we acknowledge God's presence at work in our lives.

Gratitude begets love, friendship and mercy. It helps others as much as it helps us. Gratitude has a remarkable way of coming back to the heart from whence it came.

Gratitude—the expression of thanks—is a powerful weapon. It paves a way into places where few other things could enter. It will brighten and lighten, for it will nourish us. A grateful heart is an outstanding characteristic of a truly Christian person.

We must always be grateful for the things we get from God, and we must ever remember to express our thanks to Him. He is the giver of every good and perfect gift. With the Psalmist of old, we need to say: "Bless the Lord, O my soul: and all that is within me, bless His holy name." Psalm 103:1

God has created every good thing for us to enjoy, and our hearts should be eternally grateful for the abundance of God's blessings. He sustains, guides and supplies us. His love harmonizes and enhances our lives. His wisdom enlightens our ignorance. His power strengthens our weakness. These blessings are expressed in Genesis 49:25-26: God shall bless thee with blessings unto the utmost bound of the everlasting hills.

Philippians 4:19 informs us that God shall supply our every need. God's healing power and love and mercy are proved again and again by those who stand fast in their faith.

Above all, God has provided for our souls' needs, by offering us forgiveness and salvation. He has provided all that we have or ever shall have, and, we have the assurance that His mercy endureth forever.

God's Word shall stand till the end of time—and even beyond. "Heaven and earth shall pass away, but My words shall not pass away." Luke 21:33.

God's Love

God's love is like a cooling drink
Of water for my thirst,
The crust of bread which will assuage
The ache of hunger's sting;
It gives the joy and peace that calm
The turbulence of heart,
Give music to a lonely soul
His love and praise to sing.

God's love supplies my every need
Surpassing any other.
No greater love nor greater gift
Was ever given me.
God's love is wonderful. It makes
My faith grow stronger still.
It is an all-redemptive grace
That makes my spirit free.

Christ's Example

For me, it surely was enough
That He should save my soul,
That He should free my heart of sin
And make me clean and whole.

But my dear Master loved me more;
His task was not complete
Till He, with basin, water, towel,
Had gently washed my feet.

Kindly Words

Someone once spoke a kindly word
    To me when heart was bruised,
And never knew that what I heard
    Became the crutch I used
To help me bear a heavy weight.
    It was the golden spark
Of sweet, warm friendship, mighty, great,
    Which helped me through the dark.

When one must wander on alone,
    Grief-filled, and feeling doubt;
When all the people one has known
    Are gone, and all about
Are stony stares of strangers' eyes,
    The way is hard. Lord, send
The gift that fills and purifies,
    The kind word of a friend!

By Word, By Deed

A prayer of praise
Can be a shining thing,
But any talk
With God is wonderful,
Can glorify,
Can cause the heart to sing,
Can satisfy
And make faith deep and full.

A farmer plows
His parched and fiery sod,
Knows rain will come,
And thus his trust is shown.
We must believe
And show our trust in God.
By word, by deed,
Our faith in God is known.

Golden Memories

Keep golden memories within your heart
To draw upon when days are cold and bleak.
Hold them like cherished things; set them apart
From things you would forget or wish to speak.

These golden memories will keep you warm,
So hold them dear and help each one survive
The heartless, cruel stress of each day's storm.
All fragile things need love to stay alive.

Teach Me to Share

Teach me to share Thy blessings, Lord,
    With those whose lives I touch.
I wish to share Thy love with them;
    I have received so much.

Give me a grateful, thankful heart
    For all I will receive;
Show me the way to share Thy gifts,
    Help others to believe.

Gratitude

Gratitude—a song of thanks
For the goodness of our Lord,
Whose generous heart most willingly
Fulfills His holy Word.

He is the Giver of every good
And perfect gift to us
And gratitude should be our song
Of praise and thankfulness.

Reassurance

The Lord is with me. He will ever shield
And comfort me, supply my every need.
No good thing will the Lord withhold, but yield
The best to me. He clothes me; He will feed
And nourish me. His words have grace and power
And they sustain me each and every hour.

Liberty and Freedom—
A Return to God

"Where the Spirit of the Lord is, there is liberty,"
II Corinthians 3:17

Liberty is always where God's Holy Spirit leads;
therefore, there are never two ways to freedom, only
one—God's way.

Liberty and Freedom are words that are constantly
reechoed in our day. Many who utter these words and
chant them in their "movement" songs do not even
begin to fully understand their true meaning—unless
they have accepted Jesus Christ as their personal
Saviour.

Freedom is every true believer's most precious
blessing, and one for which he must be sincerely
thankful. Like other Bible truths, the word freedom is
hard to define. It means far more than its mere

dictionary definition. Perhaps it can be better understood through the forgiveness of sins. Freedom is a word laden with wonderful meaning.

Millions of people today are seeking liberty and freedom. But what kinds are they seeking? Many of them will never reach a goal of any sort because they are unaware of the kind of freedom they need. Freedom has been available to all men ever since Jesus Christ paid the price for it when His own precious blood was spilled at Calvary.

The first step in freedom is a release from ignorance, the chief and most common cause of one's rejection of Christ. Only Jesus Christ can deliver us from ignorance. Apart from Christianity, there can be no such thing as lasting freedom.

John 8:36 tells us: "If the Son therefore shall make you free, ye shall be free indeed." And in John 8:31-32, we are admonished: "If ye continue in my word, then are ye my disciples indeed; and ye shall know the truth, and the truth shall make you free."

God also gives a positive assurance to His followers when we read II Chronicles 7:14: "If my people, which are called by my name, shall humble themselves, and pray, and seek my face, and turn from their wicked ways; then will I hear from heaven, and will forgive their sin, and will heal their land."

When Jesus was asked which was the greatest commandment in the law, His answer was: "Thou shalt love the Lord thy God with all thy heart, and with all thy soul, and with all thy mind. This is the first and great commandment. And the second is like unto it, Thou shalt love thy neighbour as thyself. On these two commandments hang all the law and the prophets." Matthew 22:37-40.

God saw the wickedness in the land over 4,000 years ago, during the time of Noah. He saw that man was evil and wicked, and that the imagination of man's heart was sinful. The earth was corrupt, filled with violence—and the result is history. God sent the flood to cover the earth.

Modern-day permissiveness is breeding a host of vices including self-interest and greed. With many people hatred and violence have become a way of life. Numerous signs point to the day when the Lord will come again in judgment of all mankind as referred to in Matthew chapter 24, verses 36 and following. As God's people, we should therefore be ready, for we know not the day or the hour when our Lord will come.

Man can destroy the kind of freedom that he has power to give, but he is not able to destroy that which God alone bestows. Freedom and liberty are not what they sometimes appear to be.

Each of us must understand that nothing can take God's liberty from those who are in the center of His will. Paul kept his freedom, despite his many imprisonments, because he was a servant of God. As Galatians 5:1 tells us, we must "Stand fast therefore in the liberty wherewith Christ hath made us free, and be not entangled again with the yoke of bondage."

The Dissenter

So loud the clamor
And my voice so small,
I doubt if any heard
My words at all.

But yet I stood
Before the angry crowd
Gave my opinion, bold
And brave and proud.

I had the courage
For my small protest;
No one could say to me:
"You failed the test."

Aggressor

A root has strength to split a rock.
    Entwined and firmly bound,
The rock must lay there passively,
    Embedded in the ground.

So can a faith be split and hurt
    By evil that comes near it;
A heart with hope and faith must fight
    All evil and not fear it.

What Men Must Learn*

Things must be labored for. Since time began
    No good and worthy thing will come by chance.
The struggle may be hard for every man,
    But every one must keep great vigilance
And keep his principles intact and whole.
    Each man must have a faith that sees the worth
Of other men; keep freedom of the soul;
    Respect the heritage of every birth.

All men must keep the faith, must ever fight
    To see his basic freedom is kept free
        And moral values never will be lost.
There may be wrong, but there is always right.
    All men must learn that their integrity
        Must be retained, whatever be the cost.

May Peace Soon Come!

It is imperative that peace must come,
That fear be stilled, that all uncertainty
Be cleared away. God grant tomorrow's sun
Bring quietness. May every kind heart see
The world's chaotic whirlwind settle down,
The awful clamor slowly die away.
May every city, village, hamlet, town
Know once again hearts joyous, free and gay!

Hour of Shining Peace

Out of the commonplace, I would prepare
An hour bright with beauty. I would share
An hour of shining peace from some far hill,
A time of quiet joy, all tumult still.

Out of the commonplace, courageously,
I'd find that longed-for place where all would be
In hope and faith and trust. I only ask
That God's kind hand would guide me at my task.

The Glory of Worship

"Mine eyes are ever toward the Lord;
for he shall pluck my feet out of the net."
                                    Psalm 25:15

True faith is a condition of true devotion. A Christian faith is a positive human response to our God as revealed in the life and message of His Son Jesus Christ. All faith results in a unity of belief and action. Faith is a conviction about life and for life.

Every true Christian not only believes in God, but also lives a dedicated life in harmony with his belief. His belief is more than mere opinion or intellectual assent; it is a full and wholehearted trust and dedication.

The Christian not only believes that there is a God, but he believes and trusts in God. His is not just an opinion or a fervent hope; his is complete trust and certainty, and his life is one of complete dedication and surrender. And, with Luther, he knows that "To have a God is to worship Him."

A Christian understands that to know God is to love Him and serve Him. When we know and love and serve God, we are worshipping Him. Worship must be selfless. We give ourselves to God when we worship. He who comes to worship God with an ulterior motive in his mind and heart, shall not find Him. Nor will he find that which he seeks. Worship is only for the purpose of glorifying God.

When we worship, it must be done in spirit and in truth. The language we use in worship, whenever language is necessary, can be in the simplest of terms. Words are often not even necessary, for true worship is adoration. God hears us even before we speak. We can adore God with the heart and the mind. We can listen to the "still, quiet voice" and know that God responds to our prayers. God knows our hearts and minds.

When we come into the holy presence of God with our worship, we often will utter that which is unutterable, speak that which cannot be put into words. We must think; we must feel with our emotions; we must speak from the heart. This is the best and greatest form of worship. An adoring love knows no bounds, no limits.

In our worship, God's concern for us must be ever uppermost in our minds, for He is infinite. Our finite, insignificant little lives take meaning when we accept the fact that God loves us and cares for us.

When God sees and marks the falling of every small

sparrow, how much more does He not see and mark the way of man who was created in His own image?

Worship stirs the heart into eager, vibrant life. It becomes awakened by the very glory of worship. The glory of God has a great and moral importance to the dedicated Christian. It gives him a sense of importance and a knowledge of his own personal responsibility. Once an individual has become aware of the glory of God in his life, he cannot retreat. He does not even wish to retreat. He can go forward, steadily and stoutly, filled with determination, vigor, and desire to accomplish a part of God's work.

When worship is sincere and not an affectation, we are moved by a sense of God's divine presence. If there is no awareness of His presence, something tremendously wrong is present within us. Our devotion to God will lack strength and power.

Our prayers must be earnest and sincere; we must seek to recapture the feeling of God's presence within us and around us; we must cleanse our hearts, souls and minds of any deterrent which may cause God to seem far away. If we seek God with the right attitude and the proper spirit of love and reverence, God will reveal Himself to our hearts.

Christian faith is a precious and vital thing. It must be filled with vision, strength, and a knowledge of the transforming power of God if it is to move us into action.

We must declare, as did the apostle Paul: "But we all, with open face beholding as in a glass the glory of the Lord, are changed into the same image from glory to glory, even as by the Spirit of the Lord" II Corinthians: 3:18.

In worship, we must each realize that it is not so much a matter of us knowing God as being known by Him. Worship is a way of understanding that we are understood. "God is a Spirit: and they that worship him must worship him in spirit and in truth." John 4:24. We are able to best know God when He knows us and accepts us as His own.

The world has an agonizing need of God and His wonderful love and saving grace. Only God is able to save us from ruin. Only He is able to speak the word of healing and of hope to our sick souls, and to reach the secret places of our hearts.

God's blessed love will bind us securely and firmly together as children in His great family. The word God speaks is always one of truth. It is one on which we may depend. It does not change; it is eternal. It is the one thing which can bless us and save us.

With the Psalmist, may we say: "He shall cover thee with his feathers, and under his wings shalt thou trust: his truth shall be thy shield and buckler" Psalm 91:4. "For his merciful kindness is great toward us: and the truth of the Lord endureth for ever." Psalm 117:2.

Prayer for Service

Keep me, God, from compromise;
     From being satisfied
With things half-done. Oh, let my eyes
     See now with zeal and grateful pride
In truly great accomplishment,
Where heart and will and strength are spent.

Keep me, God. Make me aware
     Of every human need.
And let my helpful hands be there
     When hurt ones cry. Oh, let me heed
Their lamentation. Let there be
Thy loving mercy shown through me!

The Healing Christ

Christ seeks an entrance through our every thought.
Our consciousness should bid Him enter in.
The loving hands of Christ will surely heal us,
His guiding love will save us from all sin.

If we accept His vital, radiant presence
And walk with Him along His chosen way,
He'll give us strength and courage by His power
And give us visions of a brighter day.

Temple of the Spirit

Our body is a temple of the Spirit,
Whose substance is the essence of our being.
The perfect life of God is in and through us
And molds and makes our living and our seeing.

The Spirit of our God is dwelling in us.
This Presence rules us, having full accord,
And we are free because our lives are guided,
Resolving all despair and all discord.

The doorway of our consciousness is opened.
Our being manifests a love and peace
And harmony incarnate in our being,
A strength and power that shall never cease.

Because of Love

God sent His Son ... what greater love than this?
His Son who shared His radiance and His light.
Because of love the Christ came down to earth,
Because of Love He brought His love and light.

His star gleamed brightly, leading men toward Him
And angel voices heralded His birth.
He overcame the power of sin and strife,
The Saviour of all men upon the earth.

Inner Vision

I sense dimension in the root,
    Renewal in the fallen leaf;
I hear a voice where silence is,
    Though it be quick and brief.

In span of any small bird's wings,
    I witness space and latitude;
In action, not in word or look,
    I see an attitude.

If knowledge there is meant to be,
The mind, as well as eye, must see.

In Praise of Doubters

The one who doubts before he will believe
Is not one who will fail to understand
When truth is known. The measure of a man
Comes from acceptance of the facts at hand.

The key to wisdom is a questioning.
No man should be condemned when he would doubt.
Each man should be a seeker after truth;
Inquiry often makes the truth come out.

Abiding Peace

The blessed peace of understanding
That can be felt throughout each day,
Is consciousness of God within us,
And this can never slip away.
It is a vital, living knowledge,
A soothing energy of balm,
The center of our very being,
A Spirit giving peace and calm.

It gives us strength, brings us protection
From all anxiety and fear;
The peace of God—its holy presence
Is very precious, very dear.
And manifest in all our thinking,
This Presence is a power for good;
A fountain for all life's fulfillment,
The meaning of true brotherhood.

Helpfulness

If I can put new hope into a heart,
Restore a courage to one filled with fear,
Implant new faith in one now torn apart
By doubtful thoughts repeated in his ear;

If I can put new strength into a soul
And help his feet to climb up truth's high hill,
So he may once again be free and whole,
Then I shall gladly do it—with goodwill.

I can recall how great was all my need,
A need fulfilled by Someone's loving power.
I shall be blessed and very glad indeed
If I can help some heart in his dark hour.

Sovereignty

Each mighty throne is destined for a fall,
Each jeweled diadem will turn to rust
And every ermine robe will turn to rag,
Each mighty empire turn to ash and dust.

A sovereignty is but a temporal thing
And every scepter soon must be forsworn.
One Kingdom only shall there be retained;
Forever shall remain the Crown of thorn.

The Guilty

It was not hammer, nail, or tree
That wounded Christ on Calvary;
These were the things He loved and used,
And none of these would have abused
The body of our Lord and Christ
When He was cruelly sacrificed.

Man's hatred, evil heart, and fear
Are blamed for this. The One so dear
Was hurt by man. Men cry in shame
And beg forgiveness in His name
For their great wrong. And Jesus lives
And loves and beckons and forgives.

Dominance

When men are bold
And tongues know freedom's voice,
When all men's hearts are free,
Men may rejoice.

But bitterness,
When hatred fills the eyes,
Will kill, destroy, or maim,—
And freedom dies.